Your

and s

Fortunately you only get one set of changes, in one area, at a time; if all these aspects of your life were being shaken up at once, you'd probably have to lie down for the next 100 years just to cope. If you were born between 24 September and 23 October then you'll already be quite accustomed to a feeling of buzz, excitement and electricity.

The diary supplied in your Handbag Horoscope is there so that you can keep track of all the wildness, the weirdness and the wonder. It starts on page 25. Creatively, maternally or romantically, you're in one of the biggest cycles of change for over a century. Enjoy the freedom!

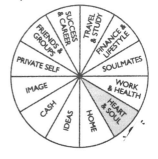

Jessica Adams
Handbag Horoscopes

libra

September 24–October 23

AN ONYX BOOK

ONYX
Published by New American Library, a division of
Penguin Putnam Inc., 375 Hudson Street,
New York, New York 10014, U.S.A.
Penguin Books Ltd, 27 Wrights Lane,
London W8 5TZ, England
Penguin Books Australia Ltd, Ringwood,
Victoria, Australia
Penguin Books Canada Ltd, 10 Alcorn Avenue,
Toronto, Ontario, Canada M4V 3B2
Penguin Books (N.Z.) Ltd, 182–190 Wairau Road,
Auckland 10, New Zealand

Penguin Books Ltd, Registered Offices:
Harmondsworth, Middlesex, England

Published by Onyx, an imprint of New American Library,
a division of Penguin Putnam Inc.
First published by Penguin Books Australia Ltd, 1999

First Onyx Printing, November 2000
10 9 8 7 6 5 4 3 2 1

REGISTERED TRADEMARK—MARCA REGISTRADA

Printed in the United States of America

Acknowledgments

When I was seven years old, I read a book called *Catweazle and the Magic Zodiac,* by Richard Carpenter. Catweazle was a magician, and he was looking for the twelve star signs. In fact, he spent his entire time rushing around the English countryside on a tricycle, hunting them down.

As I was writing each Handbag Horoscope, I was reminded of Catweazle. And I would like to thank him for converting me to astrology at the age of seven. It was much more interesting than Barbie dolls, and it still is.

Handbag Horoscopes began as a scribbled idea on a notepad. Alison Cowan, Julie Gibbs and Gaby Naher turned the idea into something real. Thank you! I would also like to thank Electric Ephemeris and Adam Smith for their help with the tables.

Contents

1. Astrology Works—and Here's
the Proof   1

2. What It *Really* Means to Be a
Libran Woman   10

3. Surfing the Stars—How to Make the
Most of the 21st Century   15

4. Dates for Your Diary   25

5. Your Venus Sign—Is This the Real You?   42

6. Profile of Your Soulmate   69

7. The Spooky Bit at the Back   90

ONE

Astrology Works— and Here's the Proof

Here are the big five arguments against astrology. You've probably heard them all before:

1. *Newspaper and magazine predictions are too general—they could mean anything.*
2. *How can the planets affect our lives when they're so far away?*
3. *Astrologers just make it up.*
4. *How can the future be the same for one in twelve people?*
5. *If astrology works, why aren't all astrologers millionaires?*

OK, get ready for the five big answers:

I write horoscope prediction columns for many magazines around the world, including *Cosmopolitan* and *New*

Woman. They are general predictions because media astrology is a general business. I only know your Star Sign, after all—I don't know your Rising Sign, or your Moon Sign, or anything about your midheaven—and these really matter.

However, some things really stand out. Because you're a Libran, I know that since 1996 you have started to see how important the issues of freedom, space and independence are in your love life. That is a general statement, based on the fact that Uranus, the planet which represents the craving for individuality and independence, has recently been in the 5th House, which is your department of sex and romance.

I can't nail it down to specifics about your love life in my columns because I don't know if you have two lovers, one in every port, a radical celibate lifestyle, a husband or a de facto partner. Neither does any astrologer. That's why we can only predict your future in fairly general terms, talking about a broad concept like the issue of freedom in romance.

It's a bit like weather forecasters. They can only ever tell you about possible showers over certain parts of your area. Because they have to take in such a large audience living all over the place, they have to make sweeping generalizations. They could probably tell you that at five minutes past one when you open your front door it's going to pour down with rain, but only if you get the forecaster over for a personal consultation!

It's the same with astrology. A personal horoscope consultation (based on the time, date and year of your birth) will be stunningly accurate, specific and detailed in the hands of a good astrologer. In the meantime, magazine and newspaper forecasts are pretty damn good. Not all the time. But most of the time. Want to hear some?

The Experiment Subject: Hillary Clinton (Scorpio)
The Event: Bill Clinton's affair with Monica Lewinsky goes public
The Date: August 1998

☆ **The Astrologer:** Elizabeth Potier
  The Magazine: U.S. *Elle*
  She Said: Scorpio—"Around the 21st, ask yourself 'Are others being dishonest or simply stupid?' Perhaps a little of both. Find your forgiveness zone and remember that sometimes happiness depends on how much you can overlook."
☆ **The Astrologer:** Marjorie Orr
  The Magazine: UK *Saturday*
  She Said: Scorpio—"There may be muddles and misunderstandings with family members

which make you panic on and off until August when you need to be firm but fair. Lay your cards on the table and insist everyone else does the same. June to September could be a cooling period with certain close mates. Saturn is pointing out flaws and inadequacies. In certain relationships this could mean a parting of the ways."

One of the things that makes a great astrology column is the smart advice, as well as the accuracy of the prediction. And that's basically what it's all about. By looking at the positions of the planets in the heavens, astrologers who know their stuff can give you time-honored advice, based on at least 500 years of testing and research by the stargazers who have gone before. They can give you insights so that you are free to make a more informed choice about your life. We call it predicting, but of course, it's only the fact that a column is printed at the beginning of the month that turns the words into predictions. Astrology's real function is to explain the present. To look at it in terms of opportunities not to be missed and painful experiences to be understood, or even avoided.

Even though you might accept that astrology works, how do you get your head around the fact that a distant planet like Pluto can possibly affect a woman down here on planet Earth?

There are many explanations of the "how it works" variety. Read *The Scientific Basis of Astrology*, by Percy Seymour, if you need to know more. Basically, what I do is just pick up a hefty book and chuck it at skeptics. They're quite heavy in hardback and make good ammunition. A skeptic, by the way, is usually someone who read the side of a Snoopy Star Sign coffee mug in 1973 and has based his entire argument on that.

Excuse me for getting a little obstreperous here. But after all, I do this for a living. And no, I don't make it up (neither does any other media astrologer, to my knowledge).

I know it might sound strange that just because you are a Libran, you can be going through the same basic life experiences as one-twelfth of the population. Think of Star Signs as being similar to gender, though, and it doesn't look quite so weird. Women have repeated life patterns: we have the menstrual cycle to deal with, just because we were born female; we also know in advance when we're likely to experience menopause; and when we get pregnant we can usually predict the timed outcome of that too! Being born under the label "woman" means you'll go through life with a higher-pitched voice, among other things. At the end of the day, astrological labeling isn't that different. It's all cosmic number crunching, and knowing you're a Libra or a Pisces, or whatever, is no more mysterious than knowing you're a woman. Based on what astrologers know about these signs, they can also make predictions for you, or talk about general characteristics.

And, by the way, there is no such thing as a cusp. You really are either one sign or the other. Give your birth details to an astrologer and they can sort it all out for you.

This knowledge is enough to make astrologers—or their clients—wealthy. And quite a few of them are (though they don't talk about it much). However, in order to make millions from this business, you have to be born with the sort of birth horoscope that leans toward you being good with money or lucky with deals. If you were born with a tricky cash chart, you can time Jupiter trines to the 2nd House for all you are worth (sorry, I had to stick some astro-lingo in there!) and you're still not going to take Ivana Trump out to lunch.

Astrology works. It's so accurate that sometimes I believe what it tells me even when the evidence is going against it. In December 1996, *New Weekly* magazine in Australia asked me to predict Brad Pitt's year ahead.

They were carrying stories about his blissful romance with Gwyneth Paltrow at the time, and photographs of them in poolside full-frontal hugs. It wasn't easy to print this, but after looking at Brad's chart, I had to do it.

***New Weekly*, December 1996:** "Brad's relationship with Gwyneth Paltrow has been formed at a time when he is not 100 percent clear about what he wants or needs. It will be tested out in 1997, when one of them will have to deal with a cooling-off period."

In June 1997 they split up.

I wrote Emma Thompson's year-ahead prediction on her birthday.

***New Weekly*, April 1995:** "Emma's love life this year looks very complicated. She faces some difficult questions with husband Kenneth Branagh in April and June."

Six months later, they separated.

Good astrologers never, ever predict actual separation or divorce—firstly on the grounds that they wouldn't want to hear it, so why would you? And secondly on the grounds that it's impossible. Clairvoyants predict specific events. Astrologers can only predict general moods and trends. If you choose to do something major, like leave your husband, that's your business. We can only tell you the emotional weather at the time and hopefully guide your decision by supplying extra information and insight.

Finally, let's be real about this. It doesn't work with 100 percent accuracy all the time. This may be because astrologers are only human and, like doctors, they occasionally make a wrong diagnosis. It may also be because of the planet Uranus, which rules chaos theory, and consequently mucks everything up now and again—and Neptune, which rules confusion. Astrologers accept that Uranus and Neptune are part of the deal, and if we do that, we also have to live with the fact that our insights will sometimes be wrong, because that's what these planets stand for—chaos and confusion! The occasional wrong call may even be part of the greater pattern that makes most of it right.

For the most part, though, astrology will work for you if you let it, and it's like weather forecasting for the soul. Did you know that most magazine astrologers have to send in their columns over three months before the issue appears on the newsstands? In year-ahead predictions we are often working a whole 12 months into the future. Skeptics and some prejudiced scientists knock us, but we are prepared to go into print, and on the record, ahead of time—every time.

Here's Penny Thornton (former astrologer to Princess Diana) predicting Bill Clinton's year ahead in January 1998, in Australia's *Who Weekly* magazine: "He seems invulnerable to anything the cosmos can throw at him and will ride through 1998's holocausts. The scandals won't stop, but if he's emerged smelling like a rose before, he'll do it again."

My advice is to check astrology, test it and use it. It's there so you can understand what the hell is actually going on when things are bad, and so that you can energetically exploit life's more fabulous opportunities when they come your way.

TWO

What It *Really* Means to Be a Libran Woman

OK. Let's start at the beginning and be straight about this. Here's what you're not—

Claustrophobic. Lazy. Indecisive.

A lot of rubbish gets written about your sign. This is because someone made it all up in about 1930 and it's just been recycled ever since. I've seen the most bizarre things about Libra printed inside birthday cards ("You're the best-dressed sign of the zodiac"). Well, that's nice for your ego, but it has nothing to do with astrology—or what it really means to be a Libra.

How does a sign get "given" characteristics anyway? It began with the first stargazers, who noticed that babies born when the sun appeared to be passing through a certain zodiac constellation seemed to have traits in common. The pattern of stars that makes up Libra could really be anything—a peacock, a slice of pumpkin pie, a pogo stick. The fact that the ancients decided the stars joined together to make a pair of scales is significant, though.

Symbolically scales represent perfect balance. And now we're talking about a connection. Because what matters most to you, and other Librans, is a sense of harmony, fairness and an evenly weighted world. That's why your greatest happiness comes from a partnership. It may be romantic or sexual—a marriage is an obvious example—or it may be a working partnership, a financial double-act or even something you do as a hobby. You can and do approach life by yourself, and through group endeavours. But to you, the most important thing in the world is an agreement with another man or woman that will put you on one side of the partnership scales, while they even up the other side. The late, great Linda McCartney found a partnership for a lifetime with Paul McCartney. And, for the record, Paul McCartney's other great partner, John Lennon, was a Libran too.

Libran Anita Roddick is married to Gordon Roddick, who is also her business partner in The Body Shop. Libran Dawn French has two partnerships—a comedy double-act with Jennifer Saunders, and her marriage to fellow comedian Lenny Henry.

If you've ever used a set of old-fashioned kitchen scales and tried to even up flour on one side and rice on the other, you'll get a firsthand idea of what Libra is all about. Your mantra for living might be, "We may be different, but together we can create harmony." If

Libra sees a lack of balance, or a lack of harmony, she tries to correct it. Don't believe this stuff about being indecisive—Margaret Thatcher is a Libran!

Libra Realities

- *You function best in a true partnership.*
- *Lopsided or unbalanced situations strike you as unfair, and your views are strong.*
- *You know how important adjusting and pulling your weight with people is.*

"Gordon and I operate on the partnership principle— he does his bit and I do mine, but we do it together, with a common purpose."
Anita Roddick, cofounder of The Body Shop, born 23 October 1942

Tolerant Libra

Two recent surveys indicate that you feel it's extremely important to tolerate differences between people. Compared to other signs, you are less easily fazed by differing religious, national and cultural customs. In fact, in one survey (recounted by Gunter Sachs in *The Astrology File*), Librans held that tolerance toward foreigners and those of other faiths was especially important and worthwhile. It seems you really do believe in balance—the Libran scales symbol is an accurate one.

Who Do You Get Along With?

It's wrong to say that you're most compatible with Aquarius or Gemini—or that you don't get along with Aries. You've probably read things like that everywhere, but in actual fact you need to have full horoscopes drawn up for you and your partner if you want to know the whole truth. A relationship or a marriage is extremely complicated, and so is astrology. That's why comparing something as basic as Star Signs gets you nowhere!

For the real story you need to see a professional astrologer:

- *Your Moon Sign will have to be compared to your man's chart to see how you'll feel about living together or starting a family. How would you deal with illness, miscarriage or moving house? Your Moon Signs describe if you're going to see life the same way and be there for each other emotionally and domestically.*
- *Your Venus Sign will have to be compared to your man's chart to see how romantic, erotic and loving your relationship's really going to be. If you want a long-term relationship or marriage where the passion never really fades, then you will need strong chemistry based on your Venus Signs.*

- *Your Mercury Sign will have to be compared to his chart, too, to see if there will be communication problems. Will phone calls be easy for both of you, or will it never feel quite right? What about clear understanding and good listening skills? Mercury Signs matter.*
- *Your Mars Sign will have to be compared to his chart to see how both of you are going to handle irritation, anger or stress as a couple. Mars also has an influence on sexual tension, and sex in general. Will you drive each other mad, or can you deal with anger constructively?*

What you can say about chemistry and compatibility is this. What you're actually looking for, in terms of recognizing something in a man which is also part of you, lies in chapter six ("Profile of Your Soulmate"). You know that "click" feeling you get with certain lovers? Part of it comes from identifying certain bits of a guy's heart, soul or brain that strongly resonate with bits of you. Is your soulmate a star, a thinker, a rock or a caretaker? Skip to page 69 right away to find out. But if you're really serious about long-term chemistry and compatibility, get both your charts compared. The Internet has several sites where you can order these, and other kinds of charts. I recommend The Astrology Shop online at www.astrology.co.uk (it has special sections for the UK, USA and Australia) as a good starting point.

THREE

Surfing the Stars—
How to Make the
Most of the 21st Century

In this section, you'll see where the major break-throughs and plus factors are over the next seven years. If you sit back and do nothing, it's possible that you'll get what you want without trying. However, if you are looking for something major, be proactive. Don't just let fate take you for a ride—double your luck by catching the wave and then getting everything you can from it while it's there. In other words, if you know you can do something more with your relation-ships and partnerships around Easter 2000, then that's the time to consciously follow up every opportunity. Especially if it involves you marrying a minor European royal, and being driven to the wedding in a pink Rolls-Royce. By the way, compare notes with an Aries. They share cycles with you in the 21st century, but at opposite ends of the year. If you're around an Aries in March–April and September–October, in particular, you will be able to swap experiences and anecdotes.

I could give you all sorts of predictions for the 21st century—job traumas, money hassles, love-life dramas or health problems. After ten years as an astrologer, though, I have come to believe that the most useful thing you can hear is the good stuff. (By the way, I just made all that bad stuff up.) What's on offer to you in this new century? Where's the good news coming from? That's what astrology is all about. Consequently I'm not going to utter any dire warnings or doom and gloom predictions. What I want to do in this section is show you how good life could be—and where the growth spurts are going to come from. The rest is up to you.

DATELINE: MARCH AND APRIL 2000, 2001, 2003, 2006, 2007

Catch the Wave: Partnerships, Problem People and Love Soulmates

You can take a more confident role in a partnership in these months. The precise nature of that partnership may change as the years go by. In some years it will be your husband or lover. In other years, your partner at work or your roommate could be the issue. An enemy or rival can be a partner, too. You have both bought into a kind of double act, just by fighting each other! And these months are also the times in your life when ex-lovers or ex-partners will be more of a big deal in your life. But in all cases, the potential for you is quite amazing.

The phrase that will mean the most at these times is "The power and the glory"—both of which will come to you through this double act or partnership. Without the one-on-one situation, you wouldn't have it, but through this person, or through this setup you have created together (good, bad or indifferent), you will find that you are able to take a leading role. To shine. And to feel both confident and empowered. You might end up in the marriage of a lifetime, or a dream romance, in March–April. Why? Because you will be with someone who lets you express yourself, and allows you to have real authority within the relationship. This is going to be quite a special person.

Let's take it to the other extreme, and imagine that you are in a hostile lawsuit with your ex-husband in this period of the 21st century. The combined forces of the Sun, Pluto, Uranus, Neptune and other planets are still on your side. Such dignity! Such confidence! What a star performance! You will impress yourself, him and everyone else who is watching (and they will be watching). And this episode will truly put you in touch with who you are, what you're all about, and how you feel about yourself. That is a gift, no matter what the actual circumstances are.

Five fantasies for March–April 2000, 2001, 2003, 2006, 2007

1. You find a lover who lets you shine and express yourself fully.
2. You divorce, and end up dispensing legal advice and relationship counseling to members of the royal family.
3. If your husband has always been the star, you'll now get the spotlight.
4. Your business partner gives you top billing or a more important role.
5. Your man's ex-girlfriend won't stop haunting him, so you get an exorcist.

Now, make up your own fantasies . . .

As you go into the 21st century you are going to get brilliant insights into what true partnership is, and how it works. You may begin a double act with someone for professional reasons, or go into some other kind of one-on-one agreement. You can appreciate the fact that you are being given space to express yourself, or to take the lead, or to "shine" in this agreement, but at the same time you are wonderfully aware of the incredible chemistry and balance that any two-person unit requires. You may even feel you're finally seeing it clearly for the first time.

If you find yourself single in March–April of these

years, do keep your eyes open. Every so often you will come across a potential partner who achieves one of two things. In the first scenario, his own confidence and authority (to do with his job or his personality) releases some of those qualities in you, too. In the second scenario, it's you who feels like Meryl Streep on Oscar night—just by being around this person. Or maybe you'll feel like k.d. lang after she fell in love with a woman who brought out her creative soul. Another aspect of this cycle is the incredible creative power it might release in you. Marry a carpenter and end up designing houses with him? Why, sure.

Enemies and rivals do come under this heading. A classic example is the man you once loved, but who left you or treated you badly. You will be amazed at how many times this kind of person reemerges in your life. Watch for the clues or triggers. The culprit(s) may not even be present, it may just be the situation around you that puts them center stage. But check how you're feeling about it all these days. Radically different? Liberated? Confident? Empowered? You betcha. The Sun in Libra will help do all this for you, in connection with the power point planets—Uranus and Pluto.

Visualize the best. Are you looking for a true partner in every sense of the word? You have a 21st-century astrological passport that says you can find this man. He may be a king or prince, and you might become his

queen or his princess. I've chosen these words care-
fully, by the way. Something about the chemistry that
takes place in the March–April cycles of the years listed
above really will make one of you feel royal.

In a few words: Focus on partners, ex-partners,
cash or work partners, lovers, rivals, foes.

Look for: A chance to find the dignity, pride, confidence and voltage you need.

If you do nothing: You'll still find yourself shining
as part of a one-on-one situation. Or if you've
ever felt overshadowed by your mate, that will
change.

If you push things: You could find your soulmate,
in every sense of the word.

DATELINE: SEPTEMBER AND OCTOBER 2000, 2002, 2005, 2006, 2007

Catch the Wave: Your Image, Your Style and Your Public Face

The sun will definitely shine on you throughout September and October 2000, 2002, 2005, 2006, 2007.
Imagine for a minute being a celebrity in the spotlight,
because that's exactly what this period will feel like.
People will be looking your way, and you will have a
chance to bask for a while. Being the center of atten-

tion sheds light on what is already great about your public face, image or appearance. And it may also show you what you need to do next. And how you can make changes or improve yourself.

It would be so easy to let your ego run out of control at these times, but I don't think you will. Having people looking your way, or having a stonger sense of your own importance or star quality, isn't going to be a problem. In fact, all it will do is make you much more strongly aware of yourself, what you are all about, and what you are here to do. You will be able to see yourself as others see you, because your name, face or image will make a much bigger impact on people. As you start to receive feedback, it will feel like having a gigantic mirror reflection beamed back at you.

This is a good time to focus on the basics of who you are, and how you present yourself. Do you need to get fitter, to gain or lose weight? Could you do something about your hair, your skin or your makeup? What about your business card, and your own web site? There are many different ways of packaging yourself and projecting an image, and while clothes or hair are obvious examples, it's just as valid to think about the sort of car you drive, or the stickers you have on the back window. What are you saying about yourself in September–October of these years?

Five fantasies for September–October 2000, 2002, 2005, 2006, 2007

1. Someone wants to write your biography—it's a total ego-booster.
2. Your hair turns green after too much swimming in chlorinated pools, but you unexpectedly start a fashion trend.
3. You lose so much excess weight that you end up being profiled in a magazine.
4. You design your own Internet home page and become a cyberspace celebrity.
5. You change your name, your signature and your business card.

Now, make up your own fantasies . . .

Whenever planets focus on the 1st House of your horoscope, which they do now, life takes a rather personal turn. As you've read, there's a lot of emphasis on your image and appearance. However, this also extends to less superficial things. What about your voice—how does that sound? What about your personality traits, especially in situations where first impressions count? Don't be surprised if a self-improvement course beckons in the 21st century.

This could lead you to understand yourself better on the inside, of course. But what is interesting is that you will become much more aware of the parts of you that the world sees. If you've never really thought about the sort of impact you make, it may be that you catch yourself in a photograph, a video, a tape recording or an interview, which alerts you to your potential. Feedback sheets from employers, or the process of preparing a CV, could also act as a wake-up call about how others perceive you.

A significant percentage of Libran women will sort out long-standing problems about their appearance or image in these years! If you are overweight, a commitment to a diet or fitness regime could not only change your image (and your life), it could also boost your confidence and self-esteem. You may even end up being asked to star at a function, or to take some other lead role in life, as a result of your triumph. It works the other way, too. If you want to fill out, you may commit to a weightlifting regime or a special weight-gain diet. You may just want to get more muscles, and so the gym becomes part of your life.

These September–October periods could find you focusing on yourself quite strongly, and on paper it may look as if you're being more self-centered than usual. But that's okay. As long as you keep things in perspective, feel free to zoom in on the way you look and feel, and how you might improve on things, or just bring your (already) fabulous assets to the adoring attention of the outside world! Sure, there will be some amazing September–October moments when you change your hair, or get a makeover, or seek the advice of a color consultant. But there will be plenty of times when you realize you were already "there" in image terms, and all you have to do is wait for the world to appreciate you. Naturally you know there's more on the inside that the world isn't seeing. But that's okay, too.

Cosmetic surgery is a possibility for some of you. So is cellulite treatment, or just a particularly inspired shopping spree where a simple thing like a new outfit or three actually changes the way you function in the outside world. Do get used to the idea of being watched, noticed and talked about. The spotlight is going to become a familiar companion to you in the 21st century. You'll be out there and up there a lot more, so you'd better be at 'em as well.

In a few words: Everyone's noticing you, so why not look and sound as fabulous as possible?

Look for: Beauticians, hairdressers, fitness experts, voice trainers, personal coaches, public relations helpers, switched-on shop assistants, self-improvers.

If you do nothing: You'll still end up in the spotlight and become more aware of your reflection.

If you push things: You could transform your appearance and become Ms. Wonderful—the object of much admiration.

FOUR

Dates for Your Diary

Jupiter, Saturn, Uranus, Neptune and Pluto are the power points of astrology. Between the dates below, you will plug into these power points as the planets make major patterns in your horoscope. A significant event may occur on just one day in the ten-day time spans below. Or you may find something gathers speed over the course of a week or more. You don't have to take Jupiter's opportunities or open yourself up to Uranus's radical changes. But if you feel something going on at these times and you can't quite get it straight in your head, this section may spell it out and help you to focus. These are really important power points in your year, so watch out for them.

Some power points repeat every year. The situation may be different each time, but the issues underneath will be exactly the same. This is why I've left space for your own notes underneath some sections. When you encounter the same Pluto power point, for example, go back to your notes from previous years. This is probably the best thing you can do for yourself in handling the future! By learning from other power point times in the past, you will know a little of what to expect, and you will also know what you did right or wrong last time.

2000
20–30 January
Neptune Power Point
The Focus: Children, love or creativity. Just circle one thing on this list.

The Issues: Sacrifice. Intuition. Spirituality. Where do you end and others begin?

Your Choice: Kindness can turn you into the star— of a creative project or interest, of a love affair, or where a child is concerned.

Notes: This power point will repeat every year until 2005. Take notes on the following lines:

_____

_____

_____

1–11 February
Uranus Power Point
The Focus: Similar to the Neptune power point you've just experienced—kids, romance or self-expression in your life.

The Issues: Honesty. Differences and individuality. Dealing with change. Space.

Your Choice: Be dignified. Be yourself. Create freedom for yourself or the other person.

Notes: This power point will repeat every year until 2003. Take notes here:

_____

_____

_____

4–14 May
Jupiter Power Point
The Focus: Joint finances, other people's money, homes or possessions.

The Issues: Opportunities. Recognition. Confidence. Total optimism.

Your Choice: You can shine now, and take the smallest opportunity and open it up.

Remember: This power point will not happen again for 12 years.

6–16 May
Saturn Power Point
The Focus: Anything from tax to business, superannuation to investment.

The Issues: Patience. Believing in yourself. Taking a reality check. Dealing with heavy stuff.

Your Choice: Express yourself, lead the way, or take the spotlight—and take the burden.

Remember: This power point will not happen again for 29 years.

29 November–9 December
Pluto Power Point
The Focus: Your written or spoken communication skills with people.

The Issues: True transformations. Power. Control. A profound sensation of change.

Your Choice: You are who you are, so express it. Change things or find your own power.

Notes: This power point will repeat every year until 2005. Take notes here:

2001
21–31 January
Neptune Power Point

The Focus: How you express yourself—in love, in creativity, or with children.

The Issue: Floating onto another level to look at things in a kind or compassionate way.

Your Choice: Healthy self-esteem makes it possible to put other people first.

Notes: This power point will repeat every year until 2005. Take notes here:

_____

_____

_____

4–14 February
Uranus Power Point

The Focus: A brainchild or pet project, your own or others' offspring, and love.

The Issue: Allowing lightning bolts to jolt you awake and show you what's true for you.

Your Choice: Why stick to old rules, attitudes or set-ups if they no longer work for now?

Notes: This power point will repeat every year until 2003. Take notes here:

20–30 May
Saturn Power Point
The Focus: Overseas or distant people and places. Knowledge and beliefs.
The Issues: Understanding what patience really is. Learning from life and other people.
Your Choice: Wisdom and experience aren't boring, they're assets to be proud of.
Notes: This power point will repeat next year—it's an ongoing theme. Take notes here:

9–19 June
Jupiter Power Point
The Focus: Broader horizons, globally, intellectually or perhaps spiritually.

The Issues: Luck—is it fate, or do you make it happen? Positive thinking. Opportunities.

Your Choice: Go exploring, and open yourself up to what's on offer.

Remember: This power point will not happen again for 12 years.

2–12 December
Pluto Power Point

The Focus: Words, telephones, books, computers—communication in general.

The Issues: Going more deeply into things; realizing that change is an intense business.

Your Choice: Confidence means never being content to live life on the surface.

Notes: This power point will repeat every year until 2005. Take notes here:

_____

_____

_____

_____

_____

2002
20 January–2 February
Neptune Power Point
The Focus: What your heart goes into—creativity, love or children.

The Issue: Feeling for others as you would feel for yourself, no matter what the situation.

Your Choice: Enlightened beings only get that way through kindness.

Notes: This power point will repeat every year until 2005. Take notes here:

_____

_____

_____

8–18 February
Uranus Power Point
The Focus: Sexual connections, your pet ideas and interests, or kids around you.

The Issues: Life (and people) can be unpredictable, and a wake-up and a shake-up amount to the same thing.

Your Choice: True freedom and a greater sense of being alive come with kindness.

Notes: This power point will repeat next year. Take notes here:

_____

_____

_____

4–14 June
Saturn Power Point
The Focus: The world outside your door, and the people, ideas and beliefs in it.

The Issues: Thinking things through with people. Being a realist. Finding patience.

Your Choice: There's something noble about doing all the right things this month.

Remember: This power point happened last year, so check your notes on page 30.

15–25 July
Jupiter Power Point
The Focus: Your career. Your studies. Your ambitions and important goals.

The Issues: Seeing the positive; pursuing the possibilities, not the impossibilities.

Your Choice: You can take something small and do a whole lot more with it.

Remember: This power point will not happen again for 12 years.

4–14 December
Pluto Power Point

The Focus: Your mind, and what it can do for you. Contacts and connections.

The Issues: Are you ready to be transformed? Or is it just your headspace that's changing?

Your Choice: A setup around you is ready to be recycled or substantially altered.

Notes: This power point will repeat every year until 2005. Take notes here:

_____

_____

_____

2003
25 January–4 February
Neptune Power Point

The Focus: Matters of the heart, close connections or creative impulses.

The Issue: Knowing that it's sometimes in your own interest to put yourself second.

Your Choice: Spiritual, religious, psychic or cosmic people or ideas could show you a lot.

Notes: This power point will repeat every year until 2005. Take notes here:

_____

_____

_____

12–22 February
Uranus Power Point
The Focus: Favorite projects and interests, life as a parent, or true romance.

The Issues: Living life in an honest, exciting, completely free way, despite the uncertainty.

Your Choice: Your confidence and sense of self fuses with your ability to accept change.

Remember: After three years of this cycle, you can now say goodbye to it—what did you learn?

17–27 August
Jupiter Power Point
The Focus: Friends—old or new. Groups, associations or circles of friends.

The Issue: Looking for the possibilities, the "yes" answers, the green lights and the luck.

Your Choice: Express yourself, be yourself and radiate! Confidence breeds confidence.

Remember: This power point will not happen again for 12 years.

6–16 December
Pluto Power Point

The Focus: Plans and lists, ideas and brainwaves, thinking, talking and writing.

The Issue: The one thing you or others can't talk openly about is the real issue now.

Your Choice: By examining a taboo or off-limits topic, you open the way to change.

Notes: This power point will repeat next year. Take notes here:

_____

_____

_____

_____

_____

_____

*(**There is no Saturn Power Point this year.**)*

2004
28 January–7 February
Neptune Power Point

The Focus: How you express yourself in close ties, or with projects you're attached to.

The Issue: What is the difference between a meaningful sacrifice and martyring yourself?

Your Choice: Put yourself in the other person's shoes—whatever their taste in footwear.

Notes: This power point will repeat next year. Take notes here:

_____

_____

_____

_____

16–26 February
Uranus Power Point

The Focus: Your lifestyle. Your health. Your work, study or daily routines.

The Issues: Being open to a whole new order. Understanding what freedom actually is.

Your Choice: Do things differently, break some of your own rules and achieve a breakthrough.

Notes: This power point will repeat next year. Take notes here:

_____

_____

_____

_____

_____

3–13 July
Saturn Power Point
The Focus: Your direction in life. Your ambitions and goals. Your status or position.

The Issues: Accepting life as it is, not as you would like it to be. Hanging in there.

Your Choice: There's a kind of glory in being open to learning experiences.

Remember: This power point will not happen again for 29 years.

17–27 September
Jupiter Power Point
The Focus: Private matters, secrets; what you do by yourself, away from it all.

The Issue: Your sense of self (and identity) will be
bound up with this.
Your Choice: Whatever has potential could grow,
but it all begins with total optimism.
Remember: This power point will not happen again
for 12 years.

9–19 December
Pluto Power Point
The Focus: How you deal with people on the
phone or on paper. Using words.
The Issues: Dealing with intensity in yourself or
others. And how does power operate?
Your Choice: Before you change a setup, you have
to change yourself.
Notes: This power point will repeat next year. Take
notes here:

_____

_____

_____

_____

_____

2005

30 January–9 February

Neptune Power Point

The Focus: The quality of your relationships with lovers and children, or your creative energy.

The Issue: Blurring the boundaries means you see what Buddha saw—that we are all one.

Your Choice: Feeling proud of yourself begins with your choice to sympathize or empathize with others.

Remember: Your notes from Neptune power points in previous years could be useful now.

20 February–2 March

Uranus Power Point

The Focus: Quality of life, quality of work, quality of lifestyle.

The Issues: Radical change. Being true to yourself. Letting a lightning bolt wake you up.

Your Choice: You know who you are, and daily life, work or health matters will reveal it.

Remember: Your notes from 2004 could be useful now.

19–29 July

Saturn Power Point

The Focus: True friendships, or any associations, clubs or groups in your life.

The Issues: Accepting what you cannot change. Being able to take a few basic realities.

Your Choice: If something about yourself is a serious matter, then take it seriously.

Remember: This power point will happen again next year!

16–26 October
Jupiter Power Point

The Focus: Yourself. Your image. What you look like. How the world sees you.

The Issue: If you think you can make it happen, then you probably *can* make it happen.

Your Choice: Recognize a lucky break when you see it, no matter what form it takes.

Remember: Read "Catch the Wave: Your Image, Your Style and Your Public Face," on page 20, too.

11–21 December
Pluto Power Point

The Focus: How you get your message across, and how you take information in.

The Issue: A natural cycle is unfolding—in-depth changes are part of this intense cycle.

Your Choice: Resurrect something. A distant connection, an idea, a plan, an attitude.

Remember: Your notes from previous years could be useful now.

FIVE

Your Venus Sign—
Is This the Real You?

Not knowing your Venus Sign is like not knowing that you're a Libran. It's just as important. Most of the time, it's actually different from your Star Sign—you might be a Libran with a Virgo Venus Sign or a Scorpio Venus Sign. Women often tell me that they feel their Venus Sign is really "them." Their Star Sign is in there, too, but it's the Venus Sign that's really accurate.

It's not surprising, really. Venus is a female planet. When you fall in love, buy clothes, put on perfume or hang out with your girlfriends, you tend to live out the personality qualities of your Venus Sign. If you go to parties and people try to guess if you're an Aries or a Taurus or whatever (how annoying!) they might get your Venus Sign, not your Star Sign.

To find out your Venus Sign, look up your day and year of birth in the tables on the following pages. These show the change-over dates, so start with the month on the left-hand side and then work across to find which sign Venus was in when you were born. For example, if you were born on 5 January 1960, your Venus Sign is Sagittarius, but if you were born on 28 January of that year, then your Venus Sign is Capricorn.

If your birthday falls outside the years shown in these tables, check out www.astro.com on the Internet—it'll give you a free rundown of all your planets.

Don't worry if your Venus Sign is the same as your Star Sign—in other words, you happen to have a Libra Venus Sign, too. It just makes you a classic double Libran! In most cases, though, you're about to discover a whole new side of yourself . . .

MTH	DAY	SIGN
JAN	1	SAG
JAN	13	CAP
FEB	6	AQU
MAR	2	PIS
MAR	26	ARI
APR	19	TAU
MAY	14	GEM
JUN	7	CAN
JUL	1	LEO
JUL	26	VIR
AUG	20	LIB
SEP	14	SCO
OCT	10	SAG
NOV	6	CAP
DEC	6	AQU

1949

MTH	DAY	SIGN
JAN	1	AQU
APR	6	PIS
MAY	5	ARI
JUN	1	TAU
JUN	27	GEM
JUL	22	CAN
AUG	16	LEO
SEP	10	VIR
OCT	4	LIB
OCT	28	SCO
NOV	21	SAG
DEC	14	CAP

1950

MTH	DAY	SIGN
JAN	1	CAP
JAN	7	AQU
JAN	31	PIS
FEB	24	ARI
MAR	21	TAU
APR	15	GEM
MAY	11	CAN
JUN	7	LEO
JUL	8	VIR
NOV	9	LIB
DEC	8	SCO

1951

MTH	DAY	SIGN
JAN	1	SCO
JAN	2	SAG
JAN	27	CAP
FEB	21	AQU
MAR	16	PIS
APR	9	ARI
MAY	4	TAU
MAY	28	GEM
JUN	22	CAN
JUL	16	LEO
AUG	9	VIR
SEP	3	LIB
SEP	27	SCO
OCT	22	SAG
NOV	15	CAP
DEC	10	AQU

1952

	MTH	DAY	SIGN
1953	JAN	1	AQU
	JAN	5	PIS
	FEB	2	ARI
	MAR	14	TAU
	MAR	31	ARI
	JUN	5	TAU
	JUL	7	GEM
	AUG	4	CAN
	AUG	30	LEO
	SEP	24	VIR
	OCT	18	LIB
	NOV	11	SCO
	DEC	5	SAG
	DEC	29	CAP

	MTH	DAY	SIGN
1954	JAN	1	CAP
	JAN	22	AQU
	FEB	15	PIS
	MAR	11	ARI
	APR	4	TAU
	APR	28	GEM
	MAY	23	CAN
	JUN	17	LEO
	JUL	13	VIR
	AUG	9	LIB
	SEP	6	SCO
	OCT	23	SAG
	OCT	27	SCO

	MTH	DAY	SIGN
1955	JAN	1	SCO
	JAN	6	SAG
	FEB	6	CAP
	MAR	4	AQU
	MAR	30	PIS
	APR	24	ARI
	MAY	19	TAU
	JUN	13	GEM
	JUL	8	CAN
	AUG	1	LEO
	AUG	25	VIR
	SEP	18	LIB
	OCT	13	SCO
	NOV	6	SAG
	NOV	30	CAP
	DEC	24	AQU

	MTH	DAY	SIGN
1956	JAN	1	AQU
	JAN	17	PIS
	FEB	11	ARI
	MAR	7	TAU
	APR	4	GEM
	MAY	8	CAN
	JUN	23	GEM
	AUG	4	CAN
	SEP	8	LEO
	OCT	6	VIR
	OCT	31	LIB
	NOV	25	SCO
	DEC	19	SAG

MTH	DAY	SIGN
JAN	1	SAG
JAN	12	CAP
FEB	5	AQU
MAR	1	PIS
MAR	25	ARI
APR	19	TAU
MAY	13	GEM
JUN	6	CAN
JUL	1	LEO
JUL	26	VIR
AUG	20	LIB
SEP	14	SCO
OCT	10	SAG
NOV	5	CAP
DEC	6	AQU

1957

MTH	DAY	SIGN
JAN	1	AQU
APR	6	PIS
MAY	5	ARI
JUN	1	TAU
JUN	26	GEM
JUL	22	CAN
AUG	16	LEO
SEP	9	VIR
OCT	3	LIB
OCT	27	SCO
NOV	20	SAG
DEC	14	CAP

1958

MTH	DAY	SIGN
JAN	1	CAP
JAN	7	AQU
JAN	31	PIS
FEB	24	ARI
MAR	20	TAU
APR	14	GEM
MAY	10	CAN
JUN	6	LEO
JUL	8	VIR
SEP	20	LEO
SEP	25	VIR
NOV	9	LIB
DEC	7	SCO

1959

MTH	DAY	SIGN
JAN	1	SCO
JAN	2	SAG
JAN	27	CAP
FEB	20	AQU
MAR	16	PIS
APR	9	ARI
MAY	3	TAU
MAY	28	GEM
JUN	21	CAN
JUL	16	LEO
AUG	9	VIR
SEP	2	LIB
SEP	27	SCO
OCT	21	SAG
NOV	15	CAP
DEC	10	AQU

1960

	MTH	DAY	SIGN
1961	JAN	1	AQU
	JAN	5	PIS
	FEB	2	ARI
	JUN	5	TAU
	JUL	7	GEM
	AUG	3	CAN
	AUG	29	LEO
	SEP	23	VIR
	OCT	18	LIB
	NOV	11	SCO
	DEC	5	SAG
	DEC	29	CAP

	MTH	DAY	SIGN
1962	JAN	1	CAP
	JAN	21	AQU
	FEB	14	PIS
	MAR	10	ARI
	APR	3	TAU
	APR	28	GEM
	MAY	23	CAN
	JUN	17	LEO
	JUL	12	VIR
	AUG	8	LIB
	SEP	7	SCO

	MTH	DAY	SIGN
1963	JAN	1	SCO
	JAN	6	SAG
	FEB	5	CAP
	MAR	4	AQU
	MAR	30	PIS
	APR	24	ARI
	MAY	19	TAU
	JUN	12	GEM
	JUL	7	CAN
	JUL	31	LEO
	AUG	25	VIR
	SEP	18	LIB
	OCT	12	SCO
	NOV	5	SAG
	NOV	29	CAP
	DEC	23	AQU

	MTH	DAY	SIGN
1964	JAN	1	AQU
	JAN	17	PIS
	FEB	10	ARI
	MAR	7	TAU
	APR	4	GEM
	MAY	9	CAN
	JUN	17	GEM
	AUG	5	CAN
	SEP	8	LEO
	OCT	5	VIR
	OCT	31	LIB
	NOV	25	SCO
	DEC	19	SAG

MTH	DAY	SIGN
JAN	1	SAG
JAN	12	CAP
FEB	5	AQU
MAR	1	PIS
MAR	25	ARI
APR	18	TAU
MAY	12	GEM
JUN	6	CAN
JUN	30	LEO
JUL	25	VIR
AUG	19	LIB
SEP	13	SCO
OCT	9	SAG
NOV	5	CAP
DEC	7	AQU

1965

MTH	DAY	SIGN
JAN	1	AQU
FEB	6	CAP
FEB	25	AQU
APR	6	PIS
MAY	5	ARI
MAY	31	TAU
JUN	26	GEM
JUL	21	CAN
AUG	15	LEO
SEP	8	VIR
OCT	3	LIB
OCT	27	SCO
NOV	20	SAG
DEC	13	CAP

1966

MTH	DAY	SIGN
JAN	1	CAP
JAN	6	AQU
JAN	30	PIS
FEB	23	ARI
MAR	20	TAU
APR	14	GEM
MAY	10	CAN
JUN	6	LEO
JUL	8	VIR
SEP	9	LEO
OCT	1	VIR
NOV	9	LIB
DEC	7	SCO

1967

MTH	DAY	SIGN
JAN	1	SAG
JAN	26	CAP
FEB	20	AQU
MAR	15	PIS
APR	8	ARI
MAY	3	TAU
MAY	27	GEM
JUN	21	CAN
JUL	15	LEO
AUG	8	VIR
SEP	2	LIB
SEP	26	SCO
OCT	21	SAG
NOV	14	CAP
DEC	9	AQU

1968

MTH	DAY	SIGN
JAN	1	AQU
JAN	4	PIS
FEB	2	ARI
JUN	6	TAU
JUL	6	GEM
AUG	3	CAN
SEP	23	VIR
OCT	17	LIB
NOV	10	SCO
DEC	4	SAG
DEC	28	CAP

1969

MTH	DAY	SIGN
JAN	1	CAP
JAN	21	AQU
FEB	14	PIS
MAR	10	ARI
APR	3	TAU
APR	27	GEM
MAY	22	CAN
JUN	16	LEO
JUL	12	VIR
AUG	8	LIB
SEP	7	SCO

1970

MTH	DAY	SIGN
JAN	1	SCO
JAN	7	SAG
FEB	5	CAP
MAR	4	AQU
MAR	29	PIS
APR	23	ARI
MAY	18	TAU
JUN	12	GEM
JUL	6	CAN
JUL	31	LEO
AUG	24	VIR
SEP	17	LIB
OCT	11	SCO
NOV	5	SAG
NOV	29	CAP
DEC	23	AQU

1971

MTH	DAY	SIGN
JAN	1	AQU
JAN	16	PIS
FEB	10	ARI
MAR	7	TAU
APR	3	GEM
MAY	10	CAN
JUN	11	GEM
AUG	6	CAN
SEP	7	LEO
OCT	5	VIR
OCT	30	LIB
NOV	24	SCO
DEC	18	SAG

1972

MTH	DAY	SIGN
JAN	1	SAG
JAN	11	CAP
FEB	4	AQU
FEB	28	PIS
MAR	24	ARI
APR	18	TAU
MAY	12	GEM
JUN	5	CAN
JUN	30	LEO
JUL	25	VIR
AUG	19	LIB
SEP	13	SCO
OCT	9	SAG
NOV	5	CAP
DEC	7	AQU

1973

MTH	DAY	SIGN
JAN	1	AQU
JAN	29	CAP
FEB	28	AQU
APR	6	PIS
MAY	4	ARI
MAY	31	TAU
JUN	25	GEM
JUL	21	CAN
AUG	14	LEO
SEP	8	VIR
OCT	2	LIB
OCT	26	SCO
NOV	19	SAG
DEC	13	CAP

1974

MTH	DAY	SIGN
JAN	1	CAP
JAN	6	AQU
JAN	30	PIS
FEB	23	ARI
MAR	19	TAU
APR	13	GEM
MAY	9	CAN
JUN	6	LEO
JUL	9	VIR
SEP	2	LEO
OCT	4	VIR
NOV	9	LIB
DEC	7	SCO

1975

MTH	DAY	SIGN
JAN	1	SAG
JAN	25	CAP
FEB	19	AQU
MAR	14	PIS
APR	7	ARI
MAY	2	TAU
MAY	27	GEM
JUN	20	CAN
JUL	14	LEO
AUG	7	VIR
SEP	1	LIB
SEP	25	SCO
OCT	20	SAG
NOV	14	CAP
DEC	9	AQU

1976

	MTH	DAY	SIGN
	JAN	1	AQU
	JAN	4	PIS
	FEB	2	ARI
1977	JUN	6	TAU
	JUL	6	GEM
	AUG	2	CAN
	AUG	28	LEO
	SEP	22	VIR
	OCT	17	LIB
	NOV	10	SCO
	DEC	4	SAG
	DEC	27	CAP

	MTH	DAY	SIGN
	JAN	1	CAP
	JAN	20	AQU
	FEB	13	PIS
	MAR	9	ARI
1978	APR	2	TAU
	APR	27	GEM
	MAY	22	CAN
	JUN	16	LEO
	JUL	12	VIR
	AUG	8	LIB
	SEP	7	SCO

	MTH	DAY	SIGN
	JAN	1	SCO
	JAN	7	SAG
	FEB	5	CAP
	MAR	3	AQU
	MAR	29	PIS
	APR	23	ARI
1979	MAY	18	TAU
	JUN	11	GEM
	JUL	6	CAN
	JUL	30	LEO
	AUG	24	VIR
	SEP	17	LIB
	OCT	11	SCO
	NOV	4	SAG
	NOV	28	CAP
	DEC	22	AQU

	MTH	DAY	SIGN
	JAN	1	AQU
	JAN	16	PIS
	FEB	9	ARI
	MAR	6	TAU
	APR	3	GEM
1980	MAY	12	CAN
	JUN	5	GEM
	AUG	6	CAN
	SEP	7	LEO
	OCT	4	VIR
	OCT	30	LIB
	NOV	24	SCO
	DEC	18	SAG

MTH	DAY	SIGN
JAN	1	SAG
JAN	11	CAP
FEB	4	AQU
FEB	28	PIS
MAR	24	ARI
APR	17	TAU
MAY	11	GEM
JUN	5	CAN
JUN	29	LEO
JUL	24	VIR
AUG	18	LIB
SEP	12	SCO
OCT	9	SAG
NOV	5	CAP
DEC	8	AQU

1981

MTH	DAY	SIGN
JAN	1	AQU
JAN	23	CAP
MAR	2	AQU
APR	6	PIS
MAY	4	ARI
MAY	30	TAU
JUN	25	GEM
JUL	20	CAN
AUG	14	LEO
SEP	7	VIR
OCT	2	LIB
OCT	26	SCO
NOV	18	SAG
DEC	12	CAP

1982

MTH	DAY	SIGN
JAN	1	CAP
JAN	5	AQU
JAN	29	PIS
FEB	22	ARI
MAR	19	TAU
APR	13	GEM
MAY	9	CAN
JUN	6	LEO
JUL	10	VIR
AUG	27	LEO
OCT	5	VIR
NOV	9	LIB
DEC	6	SCO

1983

MTH	DAY	SIGN
JAN	1	SAG
JAN	25	CAP
FEB	19	AQU
MAR	14	PIS
APR	7	ARI
MAY	2	TAU
MAY	26	GEM
JUN	20	CAN
JUL	14	LEO
AUG	7	VIR
SEP	1	LIB
SEP	25	SCO
OCT	20	SAG
NOV	13	CAP
DEC	9	AQU

1984

Venus in Aries

You don't play games, and you don't hang around. If you want to dance someone into bed, you will. If you want to punch someone in the nose, you will. Your style is playful, loud, energetic and oomphy. You're not exactly subtle (how many people have told you that?) but life is too short—and anyway, who cares? It's true that you need a reasonable amount of fire, spark or tension to remain interested in someone. You may be an extreme Venus in Aries type, too, in which case fighting will be part of a relationship pattern. If things settle down and become predictable, you tend to feel uncomfortable. You're not really into cozy coupledom, it's far too boring. The only bigger turnoff is probably wimpy love—the kind that hides behind corners and spends ages making itself obvious. You are out there and up there, and some people love it, and some people loathe it. You like instant results, fast journeys, hot music, loud kissing. You're always six years old, somehow.

What's in your bedroom? Boots or sneakers, thrown on the floor. Red lipstick.

Get his horoscope done! If he's got planets in Aries, Leo or Sagittarius—Ping!

Get him into bed: Pretend to arm-wrestle him or

pillow-fight him. Yell "Get out!" and shove him, like Elaine in *Seinfeld*.

Women like you: Chrissie Hynde, Sarah Ferguson, Vivienne Westwood, Lucy from *Peanuts*, Xena the Warrior Princess.

Venus in Taurus

You know what's valuable. It may be that antique amethyst ring you bought for a song at a country auction, or the donation you made to the Red Cross last year. You're financially secure, have an excellent idea of market values, or a strong sense of ethics which goes beyond mere capitalist fluff! You have a good eye for what's beautiful and either appreciate others' artistic talents or have a few yourself. You love the touch of human skin, and heaven is an hour-long massage. You love wool, cotton, velvet. Natural smells and substances. Real flowers, not plastic ones. Your sensuality is highly developed. You love those indulgence days they offer at day spas with champagne, facials and scalp massages thrown in. Money is an issue for you, nonetheless. Luckily you're a born businesswoman or do-it-yourself accountant. Even if you give money to charity, you still know what a loaf of bread costs. Once you find out what you like in life, you stick to it quite stubbornly.

What's in your bedroom? One beautiful, valuable object. CDs. Massage oil.

Get his horoscope done! If he's got planets in Taurus, Capricorn or Virgo—Great!

Get him into bed: Rub his neck or shoulders, let him feel your wool or velvet jacket.

Women like you: Paloma Picasso, Barbra Streisand, Enya, Joanna Lumley, Janet Jackson, Cher.

Venus in Gemini

This side of you is funny and clever. Witty and well-informed. You make the people around you smile, or just laugh, on a daily basis. You don't find it hard to network or make connections—it comes naturally to you, and you enjoy it. You swap business cards, e-mail addresses and phone numbers. You always know what's going on, and who said what to whom (and why). When life becomes too boring, heavy or embarrassing you know how to break it up with exactly the right comment, and people rely on you to do so. Friends, family or lovers make up nicknames for you, or you make up nicknames for them. You read the gossip columns—hell, you could write them. You always put the best comments on people's birthday cards. In your prime, you have run up phone bills bigger than your monthly food budget. You can't stand being bored. You can't cope with bimbos, or himbos. You're brainy and funny, and that's how you get to people. Works every time.

What's in your bedroom? Books, magazines, news-papers, telephone, notepad, pens.

Get his horoscope done! If he's got planets in Gem-ini, Libra or Aquarius—Ping!

Get him into bed: Be smarter than every other woman in the room. Be wittier, too.

Women like you: Candice Bergen, Victoria Wood, Nora Ephron (director of *Sleepless in Seattle* and *You've Got Mail*).

Venus in Cancer

You're a sweetie, but then you think other people are, too. You completely and genuinely care for people, and although you're not a saint, the time and energy you've thrown other people's way qualifies you for minor guru status. You can go too far (you know you can) and not everyone likes emotion or nurturing dripped over them. You make an excellent friend, lover or relative, however. You make people tea, offer them the comfy chair, ask them what's wrong, and give them second helpings of whatever they like. Your other great talent is making your house or apartment really feel like a home. It's not just your attention to domestic detail, design, color or atmosphere. It's because you believe your home is a place to pull people into—a kind of modern-day sanctuary, in fact. You love a family feel. If you can't get it from your own family, you assemble friends around you or create your own family later on. You need a clan around you. You need them, and they need you.

What's in your bedroom? Childhood things, gifts from people you love, .photographs.

Get his horoscope done! If he's got planets in Cancer, Scorpio or Pisces—Ping!

Get him into bed: Cluck over him a bit, cuddle him, show cleavage or cook soup.

Women like you: Delia Smith, Princess Diana, Hazel Hawke, Mary Poppins, Kaye Webb (founder of Puffin children's books).

Venus in Leo

Lust for life is not your problem. You're into love, good times and creativity in equal amounts, and you have a lot to give in all three areas. Sometimes you live your life like a film, or a television mini-series. You know you do—you can almost watch yourself, watching yourself. Occasionally, everything's just a drama in love. It's better than being bored, though. Some couples are so drab, predictable and ordinary they make you want to hurl yourself off the balcony. Little scenes are not uncommon with you, in love, at work, with friends or with the family. You also like being around people and events with a bit of an ooh-ah-wow factor. You need a man you can link arms with and look good with. Is it his talent, job, looks, cash or reputation? You adore luxury. You don't care about saving money; you'd rather have Chanel, Prada or The Ritz every time.

What's in your bedroom? The kinds of little luxuries Hollywood stars and English royals probably get for Christmas.

Get his horoscope done! If he's got planets in Aries, Leo or Sagittarius—Ping!

Get him into bed: Turn it into a little saga, give it a bit of style, suspense or drama.

Women like you: Coco Chanel, Jacqueline Kennedy Onassis, Courtney Love, Madonna, Lady Penelope, Nancy Mitford.

Venus in Virgo

If a job's worth doing, it's worth doing perfectly well. You love the details of the work you do, or the papers you pile up on the desk. Getting it right, in a precise and perfect way, is extremely satisfying. Others jam the last piece of the jigsaw into place and make it fit. It looks ugly, and you hate that. You patiently sort and file until you find the right piece, and then . . . perfection. Sex can be like that with you, too. It's nice if it's down to a precision art sometimes. You also get a lot from helping people and quietly doing things for them in a practical way. If you love a man, you probably can't help him enough. If it's a work thing as well, then even better. You understand. You don't mind getting involved—after all, if there's one thing you appreciate, it's the all-important nature of work. Because you want perfection so much, in so many ways, you can get too picky, too critical and too analytical with the poor old human beings around you—and yourself. It doesn't have to be like that, though. You love a routine, and most Venus in Virgo women have little daily rules and rituals about healthy eating and drinking.

What's in your bedroom? A clean smell, and crisp bed linen. A definite absence of dust.

Get his horoscope done! If he's got planets in Taurus, Virgo or Capricorn—Ping!

Get him into bed: Ask him about his work, offer him a practical piece of help or a useful favor.

Women like you: Miss Moneypenny (James Bond's PA), Claudia Schiffer, Shirley Conran, Lois Lane.

Venus in Libra

You know what looks good, and if it doesn't look good, you're probably too nice to say anything, but you quietly die inside. This applies to clothes, houses, art . . . you name it. Your ears are also sensitive (which may reveal itself during sex) and music moves you. You're a mirror-hopper. If you're going out somewhere important and you're not quite sure about the shoes, or the hair, or the jacket (how many times has that happened?), you hop from mirror to mirror throughout the evening. Other people don't notice—they're too busy being charmed by you. You can turn it on, and that's OK. Some people race toward conversational crashes, but you spot the danger zone ten miles before it happens and smoothly swerve everything away from the trouble spot. Born with this Venus sign, you can truly never get enough of love and romance. In your own life, in other people's lives, in films, in poems, in endless reruns of *Pride and Prejudice* on TV . . . You crave the balance that comes when people can be peaceful with each other. That's true beauty. And you love a true working partnership, either in your career or your private life. You especially enjoy it when you balance someone else out with your differences, and vice versa.

What's in your bedroom? Photographs or paintings. Wardrobe contents to die for.

Get his horoscope done! Has he got planets in Gemini, Libra or Aquarius? Ping!

Get him into bed: Send him flowers. Do something old-fashioned and girlie; wear lace or roses.

Women like you: Dawn French, Jayne Torvill, Olivia Newton-John, Linda McCartney, Susan Sarandon.

You're a Libra with Venus in Libra
Did you know that your strongest friendships and relationships will be with people whose Star Signs or Venus Signs are Libra, Leo, Sagittarius, Gemini or Aquarius?

Venus in Scorpio

People never tell you what nice weather we're having, because they sense something in your eyes that would kill them at five paces. You were made for more than polite conversation or meaningless social crapola. You are an extremely intense, emotional and passionate woman. Relationships bring it out, like the sun luring a tiger snake from its burrow. You go very, very deep with people. The love is several hundred leagues below the sea; the sex resonates inside a dark and moist echo chamber; the hatred (well, you *do* hate) is earthquake-level. Other people like boring happy endings. You tend not to believe in them. You know about the blood, tears, sweat, vomit, rage, pain, ecstasy and orgasmic highs instead. You dig deeply into life, and it sometimes digs back. You can carry too much poison, and you know it. But nobody understands human nature better. You could write a book about sex, alone. But you never would. You're far too private. Sometimes only really passionate music or poetry can contain and express the enormous power and depth of your emotions, especially where love is concerned.

What's in your bedroom? Black lingerie, dim lights, intense novels about sex, death, power, the occult or revenge.

Get his horoscope done! Does he have planets in
  Cancer, Scorpio or Pisces? Ping!
Get him into bed: Scorch his pants off with your
  eyes. Lick your lips and look away a lot.
Women like you: Marianne Faithfull, k.d. lang,
  Demi Moore, Julia Roberts, Anne Rice, Cruella De
  Vil (when you have PMS).

You're a Libra with Venus in Scorpio
Your emotional Scorpio side is led by feelings,
and this will lead you to special connections
with people whose Star Signs or Venus Signs
are Scorpio, Pisces or Cancer.

Venus in Sagittarius

You know what and who you believe in, and it could
be anything from a philosophy of life you've made up
yourself to something more formal—like reincarnation,
or heaven and hell, or socialism. You have your code,
and that's it. Occasionally people get a free lecture, but
you mean well. You're funny, or can appreciate other
people being funny. You need to have adventures in
your life, or to go exploring, to really feel as if you're
following your heart. Staying stuck in a rut for security's
sake is not you. As you get older, the search for a

sense of meaning, and for meaningful relationships, matters more. You don't like the idea that the world is some big, random place. You're always looking for the true explanation, no matter if it's religious, cosmic, scientific or spiritual. When you were younger, you typically fooled around, horsed around and fell out of bed a lot. You really adore travel, and people from other countries. The day you discover hotmail (www.hotmail. com on the Internet) is the day you discover pure heaven. How many friends or potential lovers in how many countries can you actually have?

What's in your bedroom? A travel bag that still hasn't been fully unpacked. Travel books or brochures.

Get his horoscope done! Has he got planets in Aries, Leo or Sagittarius? Ping!

Get him into bed: Tell him a joke, exaggerate a story, rave about your favorite place in the world.

Women like you: Bette Midler, Kaz Cooke, Meg Ryan, Karen Blixen, Maggie O'Connell in *Northern Exposure*.

Venus in Capricorn

There is a part of you that is so solid, so grounded, so normal and so sensible that people could drug you, dress you up in floppy bunny ears and spin you around, and you'd still seem worryingly sane and down to earth. You are particularly serious about love and relationships. It can cause you pain, but you are wise enough to know that pain is just another word for experience, and you can't have a mature or seasoned relationship without it. You like to know where you stand, basically. This philosophy guides you in love, in life and in most things you enjoy. What's the story? You have an built-in BS detector, which is why the more insane Paris fashions leave you cold, and people with pretensions turn you off. You're not particularly spontaneous or outrageous, but that's okay. Like-minded people find you eventually, and that's basically what you're after. You love success, no matter whether it's scoring points at the coolest function in town, or pulling off an amazing career coup.

What's in your bedroom? Bits and pieces from work, old or antique things.

Get his horoscope done! Does he have planets in Taurus, Virgo or Capricorn? Ping!

Get him into bed: Play by the rules of the situation, keep your dignity, be cool about it.

Women like you: Sharon Stone, Maggie Tabberer, Cindy Crawford, Tess McGill in *Working Girl*.

Venus in Aquarius

You love people and ideas which are alternative, different or out there. You're instinctively drawn to astrology, for example. You may also enjoy the Internet. You love your network of friends, and you have a lot of them—nothing too emotional, close or complicated, though. You certainly don't have a problem with platonic male-female friendships. Where love is concerned, you appreciate a relationship where you both have your own space and independence. If it feels cool, free, intelligent, feminist and progressive, then you'll go for it. You have unusual tastes and interests by other people's standards, and your wardrobe, home or haircut might reflect this. You can live with uncertainty and weirdness in your love life if it means you still get electricity and excitement. When you go to an art gallery or a shopping plaza you tend to find yourself preferring the bits and pieces nobody else likes—either that or you just walk out!

What's in your bedroom? Things that are in no other woman's bedroom on Earth.

Get his horoscope done! Has he got planets in Gemini, Libra or Aquarius? Ping!

Get him into bed: Be original, be cool, be different, be yourself, shock him a bit.

Women like you: Dame Edna Everage, Germaine Greer, Kate Bush, Gloria Steinem, Lieutenant Uhura in *Star Trek*.

Venus in Pisces

You can take emotional or physical pain away from people and animals, and that's a good thing. If you couldn't do that, you'd probably have to crawl away somewhere. You are so intensely sensitive—not only in terms of your own headspace, but also other people's—that you bruise very easily. There are two ways around this. Either you can soothe suffering away, or you simply have to escape. It doesn't have to involve a lot of money; sometimes all you have to do is day-dream, or light some incense. A complete fantasy voyage is something you periodically need to spend money on, though. Your imagination and your idealism are strong, and can get you into serious trouble with men. Sometimes the fact that you wear blinkers is a lovely thing, as it lets you accept men with all their faults and still love them. At other times you can almost feel crucified over it. A bit of balance in your life is a good thing. Poetry, art, photography or music are superb channels. You may also be drawn to the spiritual or psychic side of life.

What's in your bedroom? Impractical but intensely wonderful objects. Fabulous fabrics. Arty photographs.

Get his horoscope done! Does he have planets in Cancer, Scorpio, Pisces? Ping!

Get him into bed: Read his mind in a sympathetic way. Flutter your fingers on his arm.

Women like you: Joy Adamson, Elizabeth Taylor, Jilly Cooper, Anaïs Nin, The Little Mermaid.

SIX

Profile of Your Soulmate

Look up your date and year of birth in the tables to find out your soulmate profile. For example, if you were born on 6 January 1960, when Mars was in the sign of Sagittarius, your soulmate is an explorer; if you were born on 16 January 1960, after Mars had moved into Capricorn, then your soulmate is an achiever. If your birthday falls outside the years shown in these tables, check out www.astro.com on the Internet—it'll give you a free rundown of all your planets.

No matter when your birthday is, though, there are certain qualities you will always identify with in men. Because you are a Libran, some of your ideas about what a "real" man is are based on your Star Sign. He'll have to really appreciate the importance of a true and equal partnership, for a start. He'll have to be grounded in the basics of fairness, equality and compromise—not just with you, but with the world in general. Men who hold prejudices or who can't control their temper, or their ego, may not really seem like "true" men to you. Chances are, your ex-boyfriends or your current partner will have some of these qualities:

- *A natural ability to pull his weight in a relationship*
- *A commitment to fairness and equality for everyone*
- *An eye for beauty, especially where the woman in his life is concerned*
- *Political views which reflect his belief that justice must be done.*

To discover the sort of man who really is a part of you, though, explore this next section. Add these qualities to the traits you've just read about, and you'll begin to get an accurate picture of your astrological soulmate.

1949

MTH	DAY	SIGN
JAN	1	CAP
JAN	4	AQU
FEB	11	PIS
MAR	21	ARI
APR	30	TAU
JUN	10	GEM
JUL	23	CAN
SEP	7	LEO
OCT	27	VIR
DEC	26	LIB

1950

MTH	DAY	SIGN
JAN	1	LIB
MAR	28	VIR
JUN	11	LIB
AUG	10	SCO
SEP	25	SAG
NOV	6	CAP
DEC	15	AQU

1951

MTH	DAY	SIGN
JAN	1	AQU
JAN	22	PIS
MAR	1	ARI
APR	10	TAU
MAY	21	GEM
JUL	3	CAN
AUG	18	LEO
OCT	5	VIR
NOV	24	LIB

1952

MTH	DAY	SIGN
JAN	1	LIB
JAN	20	SCO
AUG	27	SAG
OCT	12	CAP
NOV	21	AQU
DEC	30	PIS

1953

MTH	DAY	SIGN
JAN	1	PIS
FEB	8	ARI
MAR	20	TAU
MAY	1	GEM
JUN	14	CAN
JUL	29	LEO
SEP	14	VIR
NOV	1	LIB
DEC	20	SCO

1954

MTH	DAY	SIGN
JAN	1	SCO
FEB	9	SAG
APR	12	CAP
JUL	3	SAG
AUG	24	CAP
OCT	21	AQU
DEC	4	PIS

	MTH	DAY	SIGN
1955	JAN	1	PIS
	JAN	15	ARI
	FEB	26	TAU
	APR	10	GEM
	MAY	26	CAN
	JUL	11	LEO
	AUG	27	VIR
	OCT	13	LIB
	NOV	29	SCO

	MTH	DAY	SIGN
1956	JAN	1	SCO
	JAN	14	SAG
	FEB	28	CAP
	APR	14	AQU
	JUN	3	PIS
	DEC	6	ARI

	MTH	DAY	SIGN
1957	JAN	1	ARI
	JAN	28	TAU
	MAR	17	GEM
	MAY	4	CAN
	JUN	21	LEO
	AUG	8	VIR
	SEP	24	LIB
	NOV	8	SCO
	DEC	23	SAG

	MTH	DAY	SIGN
1958	JAN	1	SAG
	FEB	3	CAP
	MAR	17	AQU
	APR	27	PIS
	JUN	7	ARI
	JUL	21	TAU
	SEP	21	GEM
	OCT	29	TAU

	MTH	DAY	SIGN
1959	JAN	1	TAU
	FEB	10	GEM
	APR	10	CAN
	JUN	1	LEO
	JUL	20	VIR
	SEP	5	LIB
	OCT	21	SCO
	DEC	3	SAG

	MTH	DAY	SIGN
1960	JAN	1	SAG
	JAN	14	CAP
	FEB	23	AQU
	APR	2	PIS
	MAY	11	ARI
	JUN	20	TAU
	AUG	2	GEM
	SEP	21	CAN

MTH	DAY	SIGN
JAN	1	CAN
FEB	5	GEM
FEB	7	CAN
MAY	6	LEO
JUN	28	VIR
AUG	17	LIB
OCT	1	SCO
NOV	13	SAG
DEC	24	CAP

1961

MTH	DAY	SIGN
JAN	1	CAP
FEB	1	AQU
MAR	12	PIS
APR	19	ARI
MAY	28	TAU
JUL	9	GEM
AUG	22	CAN
OCT	11	LEO

1962

MTH	DAY	SIGN
JAN	1	LEO
JUN	3	VIR
JUL	27	LIB
SEP	12	SCO
OCT	25	SAG
DEC	5	CAP

1963

MTH	DAY	SIGN
JAN	1	CAP
JAN	13	AQU
FEB	20	PIS
MAR	29	ARI
MAY	7	TAU
JUN	17	GEM
JUL	30	CAN
SEP	15	LEO
NOV	6	VIR

1964

MTH	DAY	SIGN
JAN	1	VIR
JUN	29	LIB
AUG	20	SCO
OCT	4	SAG
NOV	14	CAP
DEC	23	AQU

1965

MTH	DAY	SIGN
JAN	1	AQU
JAN	30	PIS
MAR	9	ARI
APR	17	TAU
MAY	28	GEM
JUL	11	CAN
AUG	25	LEO
OCT	12	VIR
DEC	4	LIB

1966

MTH	DAY	SIGN
JAN	1	LIB
FEB	12	SCO
MAR	31	LIB
JUL	19	SCO
SEP	10	SAG
OCT	23	CAP
DEC	1	AQU

1967

MTH	DAY	SIGN
JAN	1	AQU
JAN	9	PIS
FEB	17	ARI
MAR	27	TAU
MAY	8	GEM
JUN	21	CAN
AUG	5	LEO
SEP	21	VIR
NOV	9	LIB
DEC	29	SCO

1968

MTH	DAY	SIGN
JAN	1	SCO
FEB	25	SAG
SEP	21	CAP
NOV	4	AQU
DEC	15	PIS

1969

MTH	DAY	SIGN
JAN	1	PIS
JAN	24	ARI
MAR	7	TAU
APR	18	GEM
JUN	2	CAN
JUL	18	LEO
SEP	3	VIR
OCT	20	LIB
DEC	6	SCO

1970

MTH	DAY	SIGN
JAN	1	SCO
JAN	23	SAG
MAR	12	CAP
MAY	3	AQU
NOV	6	PIS
DEC	26	ARI

1971

MTH	DAY	SIGN
JAN	1	ARI
FEB	10	TAU
MAR	27	GEM
MAY	12	CAN
JUN	28	LEO
AUG	15	VIR
SEP	30	LIB
NOV	15	SCO
DEC	30	SAG

1972

MTH	DAY	SIGN
JAN	1	SAG
FEB	12	CAP
MAR	26	AQU
MAY	8	PIS
JUN	20	ARI
AUG	12	TAU
OCT	29	ARI
DEC	24	TAU

1973

MTH	DAY	SIGN
JAN	1	TAU
FEB	27	GEM
APR	20	CAN
JUN	9	LEO
JUL	27	VIR
SEP	12	LIB
OCT	28	SCO
DEC	10	SAG

1974

MTH	DAY	SIGN
JAN	1	SAG
JAN	21	CAP
MAR	3	AQU
APR	11	PIS
MAY	21	ARI
JUL	1	TAU
AUG	14	GEM
OCT	17	CAN
NOV	25	GEM

1975

MTH	DAY	SIGN
JAN	1	GEM
MAR	18	CAN
MAY	15	LEO
JUL	7	VIR
AUG	4	LIB
OCT	9	SCO
NOV	21	SAG
DEC	12	CAP

1976

MTH	DAY	SIGN
JAN	1	CAP
FEB	9	AQU
MAR	20	PIS
APR	27	ARI
JUN	6	TAU
JUL	17	GEM
SEP	1	CAN
OCT	26	LEO

1977

MTH	DAY	SIGN
JAN	1	LEO
JAN	26	CAN
APR	10	LEO
JUN	14	VIR
AUG	4	LIB
SEP	19	SCO
NOV	2	SAG
DEC	12	CAP

1978

	MTH	DAY	SIGN
1979	JAN	1	CAP
	JAN	20	AQU
	FEB	27	PIS
	APR	7	ARI
	MAY	16	TAU
	JUN	26	GEM
	AUG	8	CAN
	SEP	24	LEO
	NOV	19	VIR

	MTH	DAY	SIGN
1980	JAN	1	VIR
	MAR	11	LEO
	MAY	4	VIR
	JUL	10	LIB
	AUG	29	SCO
	OCT	12	SAG
	NOV	22	CAP
	DEC	30	AQU

	MTH	DAY	SIGN
1981	JAN	1	AQU
	FEB	6	PIS
	MAR	17	ARI
	APR	25	TAU
	JUN	5	GEM
	JUL	18	CAN
	SEP	2	LEO
	OCT	21	VIR
	DEC	16	LIB

	MTH	DAY	SIGN
1982	JAN	1	LIB
	AUG	3	SCO
	SEP	20	SAG
	OCT	31	CAP
	DEC	10	AQU

	MTH	DAY	SIGN
1983	JAN	1	AQU
	JAN	17	PIS
	FEB	25	ARI
	APR	5	TAU
	MAY	16	GEM
	JUN	29	CAN
	AUG	13	LEO
	SEP	30	VIR
	NOV	18	LIB

	MTH	DAY	SIGN
1984	JAN	1	LIB
	JAN	11	SCO
	AUG	17	SAG
	OCT	5	CAP
	NOV	15	AQU
	DEC	25	PIS

You have . . .	Your soulmate is a . . .
Mars in Aries	☆ go-getter
Mars in Taurus	☆ rock
Mars in Gemini	☆ communicator
Mars in Cancer	☆ caretaker
Mars in Leo	☆ star
Mars in Virgo	☆ thinker
Mars in Libra	☆ balancer
Mars in Scorpio	☆ depth charge
Mars in Sagittarius	☆ explorer
Mars in Capricorn	☆ achiever
Mars in Aquarius	☆ individual
Mars in Pisces	☆ dreamer

Go-Getter

- **Let's face it:** He has drive and energy. He's an action man, either at work, or on the weekends. He has loads of initiative. He's not afraid of people or situations which might intimidate other people. He can't survive without challenges to keep him going. He's masculine, in the old-fashioned sense of the word. He never gives up, or gives in. He doesn't hang around. He doesn't waste any time. In a word, he has balls. He'll never walk away from a fight or an argument—backing down makes him feel sick.

- **Why you'll love this side of him:** It's a turn-on, basically. He had the wimp part of his brain extracted before he was born. You'll know exactly what's going on with him, because he's in or out of situations so quickly. His male energy is extremely sexy.
- **Why you'll loathe this side of him:** He's incredibly pushy. Why doesn't he just let up sometimes? He can be an absolute bastard in an argument. He lacks patience and sensitivity just when you need it most. He basically puts himself first—all too often.
- **What you tell your friends:** "He doesn't waste any time."

Rock

- **Let's face it:** He calms you down. He's so down to earth about life. No pretensions. No wacky ideas about things. He takes his time. He makes life seem settled and normal. He brings in the money, or puts up the shelves, or sorts out the garden. He's like a good massage at the end of a stressful day. He understands money, but he also has a straight sense of ethics, morals and values. He appreciates fine workmanship and beautiful places and objects.

- **Why you'll love this side of him:** He's soothing company. He's in no hurry. There is something concrete, solid and secure about him. He has money in the bank, his own home or a stable lifestyle. When he tells you that you're looking good, you know it's true.
- **Why you'll loathe this side of him:** He can be the world's most boring plodder. He can get stuck in a rut and keep you there, too. He can be so into money, houses, business or possessions that you wonder if there's more to life. He's too swayed by appearances.
- **What you tell your friends:** "He's nice and he's normal."

Communicator

- **Let's face it:** You'll never be bored. He's quick on the uptake. He's funny, too. And he gives great phone, writes the best letters and lends you amazing books. He's scarily intelligent, and he can make you laugh when life gets too heavy or serious. He can usually tell you the latest news headlines, or at least the latest dirt on people. He's a mine of information, but he's never dull about it. He's fast and sharp, well informed and a natural reader, writer, talker or thinker.

- **Why you'll love this side of him:** He's entertaining. He actually applies his brain to things, and you'll either want to tape-record the phone messages or save the love letters in a bank safe. You can imagine him being switched on, funny and intelligent at the age of 70.
- **Why you'll loathe this side of him:** When he stops being clever about everything, he just sounds totally superficial and shallow. And there are times when you wish he would switch off his whirring brain and feel something with a bit more true soul.
- **What you tell your friends:** "Let me read you what he put on my Valentine's Day card."

Caretaker

- **Let's face it:** He turns houses or apartments into real homes. He has a good, strong relationship with at least one family member—maybe more. It's part of the reason he has such a caring nature. He doesn't waste money. But even so, he's into people—not things. He can be sweet and sympathetic, like a human Band-Aid. He's walking proof that you don't have to be a SNAG (Sensitive New Age Guy) in order to be sensitive. He actually cares.

- **Why you'll love this side of him:** He's even sweet when he sulks. He knows why families are important, and takes children or parenthood seriously, whether he's into it or not. He's extremely emotional, and he's more in touch with his feelings than other men.
- **Why you'll loathe this side of him:** He can become overly attached to one of four things—his home, his mother, his country or his family. To you, it just looks like he's clinging to something. His irrational moods and feelings are all emotion and no brains.
- **What you tell your friends:** "He'd make a great father."

Star

- **Let's face it:** He is respected and admired. He is a legend in his own lunchtime—and a few other people's. He has strong leadership qualities or powerful self-expression. As a result of this, he tends to shine—and also to stand out. He doesn't lack confidence. In fact, his ego sometimes blows out. He has what it takes to tell other people what to do. He may also have the ability to create, perform or entertain. He has style. He has class.

- **Why you'll love this side of him:** He's special. A leader of men, or even slightly famous. Everyone's heard of him. You respect him. He makes you look good. He's the kind of man you can genuinely look up to. And he doesn't have a confidence problem—thank God.
- **Why you'll loathe this side of him:** He can be so arrogant you want to walk out on him. And the drama! He can turn the smallest thing into a three-act play. He's quite self-involved, and wants the bathroom mirror when you do. And—yes—he can be a jerk.
- **What you tell your friends:** "He's not short on confidence."

Thinker

- **Let's face it:** He's efficient and smart. He has his home life or work life sorted out. Part of it's down to the fact that he's always making lists. But he also finds it easy to get his head around things. He's smart, he's in control. He doesn't boast about it, but he has the kind of brain that computers will never copy. He's helpful. He's reliable. You know where you are with him. He takes care of his health. He's completely responsible.

- **Why you'll love this side of him:** He's very careful and methodical, which you like to see in a man. He takes good care of his body, his workplace and his life. He's impressively intelligent. If you've been with drifters or dreamers, he's the antidote.
- **Why you'll loathe this side of him:** He can be ridiculously picky and critical, taking one detail about you, or your behavior, or your life, and treating it like a major problem. He can be irritatingly boring about the small details of life, fussing around with trivial things.
- **What you tell your friends:** "He's totally reliable."

Balancer

- **Let's face it:** He is very good at keeping your relationship evenly balanced, and will usually compromise to avoid an argument. If you ever actually fight, he won't have a problem with making the peace. His taste in clothes, music, art or homes is very important to him. He is naturally quite charming and diplomatic with people, and he's safe to take anywhere, from your parents' place to a rave. He has a talent for getting along with people—and for relationships.

- **Why you'll love this side of him:** He believes in flowers, and he actually watches the close-up scenes in romantic films. He can relate to *Romeo and Juliet*. He cares about the way he dresses and how he gets his hair cut. He also appreciates your style or taste.
- **Why you'll loathe this side of him:** This man can be the original fence-sitter, never actually expressing an opinion in case it makes him unpopular with someone. Sometimes he can seem fake, especially on a social level. Charm is fine, but he can take it too far.
- **What you tell your friends:** "Guess what he did for my birthday!"

Depth Charge

- **Let's face it:** He's a passionate man. He feels things very deeply, and is intense about what and who he loves—and what and who he hates! He has quite a bit of power or magnetism about him. And sexually inane terms like "shagging" or "bonking" don't apply. Sex is not trivial to him. It's about a deep, emotional and powerful connection which goes way beyond the physical. He's a fairly secretive, closed person. That can be quite sexy, too.

- **Why you'll love this side of him:** He's got soul. He's not a boy, he's a man. He burns for things, and you love it. He truly understands life in all its gory detail, and doesn't mind facing extreme situations or emotions with you. He's a powerful and influential person.
- **Why you'll loathe this side of him:** His dark side is ten times as black as any other man's. He can be manipulative—a real power tripper, in fact. It may come out at work, or (worst-case scenario) in his private life. He can be ridiculously obsessive about things.
- **What you tell your friends:** "Sex with him is . . ."

Explorer

- **Let's face it:** He's into the big picture. He likes travelling to other countries, or exploring the great outdoors, or getting out of the house and into more interesting experiences. He's funny, too—his sense of humor is healthy. There is nothing narrowminded or petty about this guy. He has the long view of life. He's a bit of a philosopher at heart. He's also drawn to friendships with travelers, foreigners or people who've studied quite widely.
- **Why you'll love this side of him:** You could have a lot of fun taking off to Asia or Europe to-

gether. He's game for most things. He has the right angle on life, too. He never takes it too seriously. His horizons are broader than most men's, and that's sexy.

- **Why you'll loathe this side of him:** You'd probably prefer it if he spent less time gazing at the next horizon, and a little more time on the small stuff—like security, intimacy, your feelings, and all the practical details of life. And sometimes his jokes aren't funny.
- **What you tell your friends:** "He has the most amazing attitude towards life."

Achiever

- **Let's face it:** He's a heavyweight. He's more mature than a lot of the guys around him, and he's got a wise, experienced quality. No wonder his career to date has been such a success story. He's prepared to wait for what he wants. And he's also prepared to work hard. He's straight-up and serious, and that can be quite sexy, because you will instinctively feel like getting him to loosen up—preferably in bed.
- **Why you'll love this side of him:** There's a lot to admire about this man. He gets to the top by doing things the old-fashioned way. He has a lot

of wisdom and experience, and that's something you can respect. He makes you feel safe. You know where you stand.

- **Why you'll loathe this side of him:** His ambitions—both in career terms and socially—are quite high. You could get awfully sick of watching his social game-playing with "useful" people, or hearing about work politics. You might find he's hung up on status too.

- **What you tell your friends:** "He's got it together."

Individual

- **Let's face it:** He's one of a kind. He's not very good at fitting in for the sake of it. He might look different from other people, or just be extremely different on the inside. He's exciting to be around. You'll feel a definite buzz when you're with him. He's also a man ahead of his time, in many ways. What he's into now, everyone else will be into next year. He doesn't fake it, or compromise. He's his own person, and he's an absolute original.

- **Why you'll love this side of him:** He's very broad-minded and progressive about life. He understands feminism and has a basically decent, admirable, humanitarian view of the world. He's electrifying company. And he has a dash of genius.

- **Why you'll loathe this side of him:** Mad, mad, mad. Sometimes he can be so stubbornly different and weird. If you go left, he'll go right. If everyone's going north, he'll go south. You feel like kicking him! Then there are his funny little ways—they're not always funny.
- **What you tell your friends:** "He's one of a kind."

Dreamer

- **Let's face it:** He's sensitive. He's raw like sushi. He is emotional or psychic, or both at the same time. He can relate to music, poetry, photography or films in a profound way because of this sensitivity. He's not afraid to make sacrifices for other people. And you don't have to explain how you're feeling to him—he just seems to know instinctively. He can't handle too much reality. He needs to drift off, dream or escape.
- **Why you'll love this side of him:** At last, a man with feelings! He's hard to catch or pin down sometimes, but like a half-remembered song, you'll be happily haunted by him. He's kind and

compassionate. He can feel for a hurt woman, or a hurt butterfly. He's soft inside.

- **Why you'll loathe this side of him:** You know that song "Reality Used to Be a Friend of Mine"? You can probably relate to it if you're with this guy. Drink or drugs may not bring out the best in him. But his worst faults are vagueness, hopelessness and chaotic life mess!
- **What you tell your friends:** "He feels what I'm feeling."

SEVEN

The Spooky Bit at the Back

Over the years, my job as an astrologer has given me the chance to explore other New Age ideas as well. Some of them work, some of them don't. I met Shirley MacLaine once. I asked her if there was anything in the New Age she didn't believe. She shook her head and said she believed in *everything*. I don't. But here are some quick tips and spooky solutions that I've road-tested over the last ten years. They've got nothing to do with astrology, but they really work!

Feng Shui Your Bedroom

Have you been waiting on money for months? Is someone at work driving you insane? Do you want to go to Morocco but have no idea how you'll manage it? Try feng shui (say it "fong-shoy").

You can feng shui your whole house or apartment if you wish, but for a quick fix, begin with your bedroom. The first thing you will need to do is get rid of any mess, junk or unwanted objects. Here are some classic examples:

- *Clothes that need mending that you've shoved under the bed*
- *Dead or dying plants*
- *Photos of ex-boyfriends, old letters, receipts, bills and other bits of paper*
- *Compact discs or tapes you never play*
- *Magazines and newspapers*
- *Books you've never got around to reading*
- *Unwanted presents you feel guilty about throwing out*
- *Empty perfume bottles, half-empty jars of moisturizer*
- *Keys belonging to houses, apartments and cars from years ago*
- *Rolled-up posters in the corner.*

Karen Kingston, author of *Clear Your Clutter With Feng Shui* and *Creating Sacred Space With Feng Shui*, is an expert on this stuff. If you'd like to go the whole hog, and also clear the old vibes and stale energy from your bedroom, use her special rituals—which include clapping, ringing bells, lighting candles, burning incense, sprinkling holy water and offering flowers and prayers.

For more information on this, see Karen's web site at
www.spaceclearing.com.

The general idea of starting with a clean, uncluttered
space is very important to feng shui. There is no point
in sticking a crystal in your money corner if it's going
to sit there with an old pet rock and a 1982 *Dynasty*
calendar. Be ruthless with every object in your room.
Here's what to do:

1. *Look at it.*
2. *Does it bring your energy down or up?*
3. *If it brings you down, imagine the accumulated "sag-
   ging" effect of seeing this thing ten times a day, 365
   days a year.*

It may be the only photograph you have of the guy you
spent two years of your life with, but if every time you
see it you feel an energy drop, rip it up.

After the de-junking comes the boring bit. The vacu-
uming, the mending and the window-washing. Then
comes the slightly more interesting bit—visual cleaning.

Sit on the floor. Imagine a dazzling white light pouring
in through the light fixture on the ceiling, and filling
the entire room. This is your universal cleaner. More
powerful than Mr. Clean, it's superb for obliterating old
vibes, bad vibes, and indifferent vibes. Make sure the
light is as bright, white and pure as you can make it.

Make sure you see it going under the bed and into the corners.

When you've finished, open the windows wide. You have just moved an awful lot of stuck, stale bedroom energy. A few people have told me that wonderful and strange things start happening just on the strength of this junk-chuck, cleanup and white-light exercise. Phones ring with job offers. Badly behaved boyfriends turn up with flowers. Party invitations land in the mailbox.

Now for the fun part. Look at the plan of your bedroom on the next page.

What area of your life do you want to focus on? That's where you decorate, put flowers, light candles, burn incense or aromatherapy oil. That's where you hang a picture or photograph of something that makes you happy, or something which sums up what you'd like to see happening.

You can also do some problem-solving by avoiding the big feng shui no-nos:

1. *Don't have your feet pointing at the door from the bed.*
2. *Don't have a mirror facing you when you're in bed.*
3. *If there's a fan in the room, move your bed so you're not sleeping under the blades.*

money	fame	love
💰	✴	♡
family	health	creativity
🏠	🍎	💡
knowledge	career	friends
👓	📷	👥

◀ The doorway is on this side of your room ▶

People tie themselves into knots if their bedroom isn't a neat square or oblong. If you have a corner of the room missing (in an L-shaped bedroom, for example) don't panic. Just do what you can to dress up where that corner should be. If your money corner is missing, that's where you could put a beautiful vase on the floor, and fill it with the best flowers you can afford every week. If your love corner is missing, put a rose quartz crystal in there. Some people hang mirrors on the wall of the L-shaped bit to give the illusion that the space really does extend.

It's all about using your imagination, and your common sense. If you don't want to be single, don't put up a Picasso print of a single woman in your love corner!

I've known people to see results on the same day, and other people within a few weeks. I sorted out my office and moved stacks of my first novel, *Single White E-mail*, out of cardboard boxes and into my creativity corner. The book had dropped off the best-seller lists two months previously and I honestly thought that its time was over, which is probably why I'd stashed it away in boxes. Within three days of putting it in pride of place in my creativity corner, it zoomed back onto the best-seller list at number six.

Start small, with your bedroom. If good things begin to happen for you, I recommend you go all the way and do your entire house and garden, or your apartment. Karen Kingston and Lillian Too have both written great books on the subject.

Call a Psychic Cab

This works for me about nine times out of ten. You may find it happens ten times out of ten for you! The next time you are desperate for a cab, stand on the curb and send this silent message out into the streets:

"I am (here) and I want to go (there). I have (x) dollars. I can wait for (x) minutes."

This works if it's raining, if everybody is lining up on the road in front of you, and even if it's 3 P.M. and there are no cabs on the road. Once, I didn't get a cab within my specified time (five minutes) but a friend "happened" to drive past and gave me a lift instead. It helps if you visualize the cab pulling up in front of you, and you happily getting in.

Take an Aura Shower

This is good if you're feeling tired, stressed out, ill or otherwise fed up. If you do it properly you will feel the following within twenty minutes—

- *Peace of mind*
- *Mild bliss*

I have watched people do this experiment, and some of them start smiling for no apparent reason. Other people have told me that they settle down and feel a bit more normal about life when they try it.

Lie down on the bed, or on the floor. Flop. Take

three deep breaths. Flop again. Don't feel stupid or anxious about this. It's easy. Next, say these words in your head: "What color do I need?" The rule for this is—first thought, best thought! Don't agonize over it. Zoom in on the precise shade of that color. If you chose blue, do you mean turquoise blue, or deep purple-blue?

Imagine that you have amazing rings on all your fingers, inlaid with jewels in that color. See yourself wearing that color. Take a bath in it. Feel it inside your body, as well as outside it. Stay with the color for as long as you like. This is when some people start smiling involuntarily, while others find themselves letting out a long sigh, much to their surprise. This is a sign that the aura shower is working.

Ask again: "What color do I need?" If nothing comes up, you only needed one color to correct your aura, and you can get up and carry on with your day. But you may get another color, and another color, and so on. Continue until you feel you're finished.

Wish Books

Buy a notebook you really like. On a separate piece of scrap paper, write down a list of what you would like to happen in your life. Put in a lot of details. If you want to sketch something to show what you mean, then do that. Really think about what you're after. If you want a man who has a hairy chest and a wooden leg, write it down. Nobody else is going to see this, so what have you got to lose?

Using the scrap paper gives you a chance to be absolutely sure about what you want when you finally glue things, write things or draw things in your wish book. This is a special book, which will help to bring many (if not all) of your wishes about. So keep it clean, make sure it looks great, and hide it in a safe place.

Some people cut out photographs from magazines and stick them in their wish books. Others draw what they want. Feel free to add some of the details or notes you worked out on your scrap paper.

The rule with wish books is, if it's for the good of you and the people around you, it will probably happen. What you're after is a win-win situation. Let's say you've cut out a picture of Nelson Mandela (for his integrity) and a picture of Brad Pitt (for his dimples), in your quest to dream up the ideal man. If a guy like this happens to be out there and also looking for someone like you, you'll meet.

If, on the other hand, your boyfriend has dumped you for no sensible reason, and you cut out a picture of a piranha fish and paste it over a photo of his groin, it's probably not going to happen. Win-win works. Win–

groin mutilation tends to do nothing except create bad karma for you.

Here's a list of some of the things that have been wished into existence over the years—by people I know, and sometimes by me. Next to each real-life wish book example, I've written the time it took to come true.

- *A white beach house with blue and white tiles on the porch, and a rocking horse in the children's bedroom. (This was cut out of a magazine. It took eight months for the house and the rocking horse to arrive. The blue and white tiles didn't make it, though!)*
- *A pair of black leather pants like Jim Morrison's. (These were found on a market stall about a week later. A classic win-win, as the guy who was selling the pants thought he'd never get rid of them.)*
- *A fun romance in America. (This person got the fun, the romance and America almost two years after drawing a picture of it, complete with love hearts and the Statue of Liberty.)*
- *A career with radio, TV, money, creativity and freedom. (I actually drew this for a friend and she e-mailed me two weeks later with this subject header—!!!!!!!!!!!— to tell me it had happened.)*
- *Two golden retriever puppies with pink ribbons round their necks. (OK, I admit it, I cut this out of a maga-*

zine and put it in my wish book. About three months later, I was walking past the local noticeboard and saw an advertisement asking for someone with spare time to walk a golden retriever. I did, and Max became one of my favorite canines in the whole world.)

This last example shows something else about wish books—you might get part of the wish, rather than all of it, or it may come about in a surprising way.

Computer Magic

If you have a screen-saver that allows you to make up a sentence and put it on your computer, don't waste it. You can use the same idea behind the wish book, and write down something that you would like to see happen—then watch it roll across your screen on a regular basis. I typed in this sentence in bright pink: PARIS IN THE SPRING. I found myself there last year, so it was definitely worth the effort.

People always ask me how this stuff works. I really don't know, but when you consciously decide to take something out of your head and write it down, draw it, or cut it out and stick it in a book, the universe shifts. It works the other way, too. If you wander around with these ideas in your head—

- *I'm going to have to be lucky to pass my exam*
- *I'm hooked on cigarettes*
- *I always get the weirdos*

—well, does anything ever change?

The only rule with computer magic is your frame of mind when you program your sentence into the machine. If you feel pessimistic, uncertain, silly or embarrassed, it won't work. The best attitude is either: total belief that it's going to happen one day, though you have no idea how; or The Doris Day Approach—what will be, will be. In other words, it would be great if you got what you wanted, but you're not going to sink into despair if it doesn't happen.

The wish book win-win principle also applies to computers. If what you want is fine by other people as well as you, then it stands a better chance of happening. Giving up smoking is a good example—unless you're married to the head of Benson and Hedges, I guess.

Name Your Car

The chicks at Penguin Books swear by this and so do I. If you have trouble with mechanical or high-tech objects—like cars, faxes, computers, laptops, microwave ovens, modems, plug-in aromatherapy burners and so on—name them. Mean what you say. Take your time to choose the name. Use it to communicate with your little mechanical or digital friend frequently. When I was having hassles with my laptop (the screen was wobbling and I was stuck in the country, far away from technical support), I gave it a name. Little Miranda. (The big computer is called Big Miranda.) I talked to Little Miranda and asked her to work for me. She stopped wobbling.

Reading Pizzas

Do you want to see into the future? If tarot cards are a problem for you, and your dreams just aren't predictive, try pizza reading.

First, ask your question. Your psychic side will answer it for you, using symbols, images and ideas which you will see in the pizza. What you see in the cheese, the pepperoni and the mushrooms will be personal to you. If, for example, you see a door key, and that reminds you of your roommate who is always forgetting his key, then that is a reference to him. Let your brain "bounce" around images and ideas in a dreamy way. Make sure you write it all down, though. Time may well reveal that you have answered your own question about the future by what you saw on the day you did your pizza reading.

You can also read clouds. I did it on a long and

boring flight from London to Moscow. The question I asked was, "What will I find when I get to Moscow? What experiences will I have?" After a few minutes of staring at the clouds, I wrote down this:

- *A man with a birthmark on his face*
- *Little kids with Hare Krishna ponytails*
- *Lots of dogs*

When we got to Moscow Airport, a man with a port wine birthmark on the left side of his face took our passports. I met the dogs the same night—a pack of hungry mongrels hanging around the hotel trash cans (they howled every night for a week, so they really were a major feature of my stay). The little kids with the Hare Krishna ponytails turned up on the second to last day. They were in front of me in the line for the ATM. Try cloud reading next time you fly—especially if they're not serving pizza.

Get Back to Me on This One

To finish the book, I'd like to try an experiment. Have you got a pen in your bag? Good. Look around the room, or the train, or the bus, or the plane (but hopefully not the car—this is a non-driving exercise).

Let your eyes settle on the first thing you see. It may be something quite boring, like a TV set, or quite detailed, like a piece of embroidery. Even a teacup will do.

Allow yourself to float off. What does this object or thing in front of you bring to mind? Without thinking too hard, write down your impressions in the space that follows—

Don't edit yourself. If you're staring at a manila folder and it reminds you of your teacher at school with a beer gut, who reminds you of Foster's, which reminds you of foster homes, which reminds you of stray dogs, which reminds you of wanting to be a vet, then put it all down.

Now, turn this page upside down.

You have just answered the question "What happy choices are in store for me in the 21st century?"

If you are astounded (or if it comes true), I'd like to hear about it.

Please e-mail me at this address: jessica@zip.com.au.

And have a great millennium!